The Green Technology Revolution

I0466862

Available Items and Opportunities

Taylor Royce

Copyright © 2024 Taylor Royce

All rights reserved.

DEDICATION

To all the dreamers, doers, and proponents of a more environmentally friendly future those who work tirelessly to use technology to improve the sustainability of our planet. We are all inspired by your commitment to achieving a harmonious balance between advancement and preservation. This book is dedicated to those trailblazers who think that green technology has the potential to create a more promising future for future generations.

CONTENTS

ACKNOWLEDGMENTS

Many people and organizations provided assistance, direction, and inspiration that would not have been possible to achieve with this book, ***The Green Technology Revolution: Available Items and Opportunities.***

Above all, I would like to express my sincere gratitude to the researchers, industry leaders, and specialists in green technology who so kindly contributed their knowledge and thoughts. Your innovative efforts and commitment to sustainability have greatly influenced the content of this book.

I owe a debt of gratitude to my peers and coworkers for their supportive and constructive criticism during the writing process. Your helpful criticism and unfailing support have been invaluable in helping this novel come to fruition.

We especially salute the environmental activists and campaigners whose fervor and dedication to a sustainable future keep spurring progress. Your work has served as motivation and inspiration.

I also want to thank my family and friends for their support, as their tolerance and comprehension have been invaluable during this process. Your support and faith in our endeavor have been a never-ending source of inspiration.

Your skill and meticulous attention to detail, along with the hard work of the committed team of professionals who helped with the editing, design, and production of this book, have made it a success. I appreciate all of your effort and dedication.

Lastly, I would like to thank all of the readers for taking an interest in the green technological revolution and picking up this book. Your involvement in these concepts and advancements is essential to advancing sustainable technology in the future. I hope this book motivates you to help create a more sustainable and greener planet.

DISCLAIMER

The Green Technology Revolution: Available Items and Opportunities contains content that is intended solely for general informative purposes. Although every effort has been taken to ensure that the content is accurate and complete, the publisher and author disclaim any express or implied representations or warranties regarding the availability, accuracy, suitability, or completeness of the information, products, services, or related graphics in the book for any purpose, nor the completeness, accuracy, reliability, or suitability of the information for any purpose.

Any firm, technology, or product mentioned in this book is not meant to be endorsed or recommended. The descriptions and assessments of green technology are predicated on data that is currently available and may evolve over time. Before making any decisions about the purchase or use of green technology, readers are urged to do independent study and consult experts.

The publisher and author disclaim all liability for any loss or damage resulting from using this book, including but not limited to consequential or indirect loss or damage, loss or damage from data loss or profit loss.

This book's thoughts and opinions are entirely the author's own and may not represent the perspectives of any organizations or other entities mentioned.

You understand and accept these terms and conditions by using this book.

CHAPTER 1

COMPREHENDING THE REVOLUTION IN GREEN TECHNOLOGY

1.1 The Increasing Concern for the Environment

More than just a fad, the world is moving toward sustainability as an essential reaction to the growing environmental problems. The way businesses operate and how consumers behave are both significantly impacted by this development.

- **Increasing Conscience:** The necessity for sustainable practices has become more widely recognized due to factors such as pollution, deforestation, and climate change. In order to raise awareness, documentaries, media coverage, and educational initiatives have been crucial.

- **Actions by Consumers:** Consumers today are more concerned about the environment and want brands to be transparent and sustainable. In order to retain client loyalty, this change has compelled businesses to implement green processes and provide ecologically friendly products.

- **Regulatory Difficulties:** Governments all across the world are enforcing more stringent environmental laws, which forces businesses to lower their carbon footprints and embrace sustainable methods. Investment and innovation in green technology are being propelled by these restrictions.

- **Enterprise Liability:** Companies are starting to understand how important corporate social responsibility (CSR) is. These days, corporate strategies are not complete without consideration for sustainability, which affects everything from product design to supply chain management.

- **Financial Elements:** Even though they require early investments, sustainable practices frequently result in long-term cost savings. Significant cost savings can be achieved through resource optimization, waste reduction, and energy-efficient technology.

1.2 Technology's Part in the Fight Against Climate Change

When it comes to solving environmental issues and lessening the effects of climate change, technological breakthroughs are crucial. These developments are in a number of industries, such as manufacturing, transportation, energy, and agriculture.

- **Sustained Energy:** Hydroelectric power, wind, and solar technologies are essential for lowering dependency on fossil fuels. Renewable energy sources are becoming more and more viable due to developments in energy storage, such as better battery technologies.

- **Energy Efficiency:** Building automation systems, smart grids, and energy-efficient appliances all contribute to the optimization of energy use, which lowers greenhouse gas emissions and waste.

- **Sustainable Transportation:** New developments in public transportation infrastructure, electric vehicles (EVs), and hydrogen fuel cells are revolutionizing the transportation industry by lowering emissions and reliance on fossil fuels.

- **Technology in Agriculture:** The environmental effect of food production is being lessened by genetically modified crops, precision agriculture, and vertical farming, which increase agricultural sustainability and efficiency.

- **Waste Management:** New developments in biodegradable materials, recycling, and waste-to-energy technologies are tackling waste management issues and advancing the circular economy.

1.3 What Is Sustainable Technology?

Green technology, also known as sustainable technology, is defined by a number of fundamental ideas and standards that are meant to reduce negative effects on the environment and to support long-term ecological balance.

- **Resource Efficiency:** Sustainable technology places a high priority on using energy, water, and raw materials as efficiently as possible. This idea places a strong emphasis on cutting waste and increasing output.

- **Limited Effect on the Environment:** Green technology goods are made with as little detrimental impact on the environment as possible at every stage of their lifecycle, from manufacturing to disposal. Reducing emissions, pollution, and habitat damage are all part of this.

- **Sustainability:** Renewable resources, like solar and wind energy, are naturally regenerated and do not deplete finite resources. This is why sustainable technologies frequently make use of them.

- **Lifecycle Evaluation:** A thorough life cycle assessment assesses a product's environmental impact from the beginning to the conclusion of its useful life. This method makes sure that sustainability is taken into account at every step, including extraction, manufacture, usage, and disposal.

- **Eco-Friendly Design:** Green technology integrates sustainable materials, modularity, and recyclability as well as other eco-friendly design concepts. This method guarantees that items are made with lifespan and the least possible impact on the environment in mind.

- **Civic Responsibilities:** Sustainable technology also takes into account the social effects of its use, encouraging ethical material procurement, community involvement, and fair labor standards.

1.4 Green Technology's Economic Potential

Due to the large investment in environmental projects and the growing demand for sustainable solutions, the green tech sector offers major economic potential.

- **Market Expansion:** With industries like renewable energy, electric vehicles, and sustainable agriculture growing at previously unheard-of rates, the green tech business is rising quickly. Regulation requirements and customer demand are the two main drivers of this increase.

- **Opportunities for Investment:** Venture capital, private equity, and government funding are drawn to green tech because it presents profitable investment prospects. A growing number of investors are realizing that sustainable technologies have the potential to yield significant rewards.

- **Creation of the Job**: New job possibilities are being created by the green tech revolution in a number of industries, including manufacturing, engineering, research & development, and sales. The development of jobs is essential to the sustainability and growth of the economy.

- **Competitiveness and Innovation:** Businesses that make green technology investments frequently obtain a competitive advantage, spurring innovation and enhancing their standing in the market. Improved consumer loyalty and brand reputation can result from sustainable business strategies.

- **Reduction in Cost:** Over time, using sustainable technologies can save a substantial amount of money. Optimizing resources, cutting waste, and implementing energy-efficient systems all help to save operating costs and increase profitability.

- **Incentives from Government:** To promote the use of green technologies, numerous countries provide tax exemptions, subsidies, and other incentives. These incentives hasten the shift to a sustainable economy while lessening the financial load on companies.

A thorough analysis of the factors that are propelling the green tech revolution, how technology can be used to solve environmental issues, what constitutes sustainable technology, and the substantial economic potential it contains are all necessary to comprehend the movement. This comprehensive viewpoint emphasizes how crucial sustainable behaviors are to creating a resilient and prosperous future.

CHAPTER 2

A CLOSER LOOK AT ECO-FRIENDLY DEVICES

2.1 Conscious Consumerism's Ascent

Recent years have seen a sharp increase in customer demand for sustainable products, which is indicative of a larger trend towards conscious consumption. This movement has a significant impact on markets and the tactics used by companies.

- **Better Knowledge:** Thanks to media attention, social media, and educational programs, consumers are more aware of the environmental effects of the products they buy. This knowledge affects purchasing decisions, giving eco-friendly products priority.

- **Request for Openness:** Consumers of today demand transparency from brands on their sustainability policies. This covers information on product source, production procedures, and environmental impact. Businesses that make this information available foster loyalty and confidence.

- **Modifications to Market Dynamics:** The market's dynamics have changed due to the desire for sustainable products. Eco-friendly substitutes for conventional items are replacing them, opening up new avenues for firms to innovate and serve this expanding market sector.

- **Effect on Image of Brand:** Nowadays, a crucial element of brand identification is sustainability. Businesses with a reputation for being environmentally conscientious draw eco-aware customers, which boosts their brand recognition and competitive edge.

- **Compliance with Regulations:** Regulations that encourage sustainability are being implemented by governments more frequently. Companies are making adjustments to conform to these rules, which frequently match consumer demands for goods that are ecologically friendly.

2.2 Eco-Friendly Device Types

There are many different kinds of eco-friendly devices, and each one makes a distinct contribution to sustainability. These goods are made to satisfy customer needs with the least possible negative impact on the environment.

- **Mobile phones:** Eco-friendly cell phones have long-lasting construction, energy-efficient parts, and ecological materials. Companies that lead the industry in modular designs that cut down on electronic waste are Fairphone.

- **Dwelling Appliances:** Appliances in homes that use less energy and water include dishwashers, washing machines, and refrigerators. Smart home systems are one example of an innovation that optimizes energy use and lessens environmental impact.

- **Wearable Tech:** Eco-friendly materials and

energy-efficient technology are used in sustainable wearables, such as fitness trackers and smartwatches. Certain gadgets even employ solar energy or mechanical energy for charging.

- **Individual Transport:** As environmentally friendly substitutes for conventional forms of mobility, electric bikes, scooters, and hoverboards are available. These devices encourage sustainable urban mobility while lowering carbon emissions.

- **Resources for Energy:** Energy-saving devices like lightbulbs and portable solar chargers help reduce energy use. These goods encourage the use of renewable energy sources and lessen reliance on fossil fuels.

2.3 Manufacturing and Materials

Reducing the environmental impact of eco-friendly electronics is mostly dependent on the materials and manufacturing processes employed. Businesses are embracing sustainable practices more and more in order to meet the demands of their customers and comply with laws.

- **Sustainable Materials:** Recycled, biodegradable, or sustainably sourced materials go into making eco-friendly devices. Bamboo, organic cotton, and recycled plastics are a few examples. These materials decrease waste and lessen the depletion of resources.

- **Responsible Purchasing:** Businesses are making sure that materials come from ethical sources, staying away from conflict minerals, and encouraging fair labor standards. This strategy encourages supply chain sustainability and social responsibility.

- **Manufacturing with Energy Efficiency:** The primary goal of sustainable manufacturing methods is to lower emissions and energy usage. Methods include utilizing green manufacturing processes, streamlining production lines, and employing renewable energy sources are typical.

- **Reduction of Waste:** Reducing waste in the manufacturing process is a crucial component of sustainable manufacturing. Businesses are implementing eco-friendly packaging, recycling industrial waste, and lean manufacturing techniques.

- **Alchemical Administration:** Reducing the amount of dangerous chemicals used in production processes safeguards human health and the environment. Businesses are switching to non-toxic substitutes and making sure that chemical waste is disposed of properly.

2.4 Sustainability in Design

When designing devices with sustainability in mind, circular economy principles and the product's whole lifecycle are taken into account. This method guarantees that products are eco-friendly from the point of manufacture to the point of disposal.

- **Product Lifecycle:** From raw material extraction to

end-of-life disposal, sustainable design takes the environment into account at every stage of the product life cycle. Opportunities to lessen the environmental impact are identified with the aid of this comprehensive viewpoint.

- **Separate Structure:** Modular devices make recycling, upgrading, and repairs simple. This increases the product's lifespan and decreases electronic waste. Modular computers and cellphones are two instances of this strategy.

- **Sustainability:** When things are designed with recyclable materials, their ability to be processed effectively at the end of their useful life is guaranteed. Effective recycling requires easy disassembly and clear labeling.

- **Efficiency of Energy:** The design of devices that incorporate energy-efficient technology and components uses less energy when in use. This objective is aided by features like effective batteries and low-power modes.

- **Red-handed Economy:** Achieving a circular economy requires designing items that are recyclable, reusable, or repaired. By reducing waste and enhancing resource efficiency, this strategy establishes a closed-loop system for materials.

- **Eco-Friendly package**: Environmental effect is lessened by sustainable package design. Reusable, recyclable, or biodegradable packaging materials reduce pollution and waste.

Examining the rise of conscious consumption, investigating different kinds of sustainable tech items, evaluating the usage of eco-friendly materials and manufacturing techniques, and placing a strong emphasis on design for sustainability are all necessary to comprehend eco-friendly electronics. All of these factors work together to promote the creation and use of devices that help ensure a sustainable future.

CHAPTER 3

FUTURE-PROVIDING RENEWABLE ENERGY DEVICES

3.1 Devices for Solar Power

Solar power devices collect solar energy and can be used for everything from small devices to large-scale residential energy systems. These devices offer an environmentally friendly substitute for conventional power sources, lowering carbon emissions and fostering energy independence.

- **Solar Power Sources**: For charging smartphones, tablets, and other tiny gadgets, portable solar chargers are quite common. These chargers are perfect for outdoor activities and emergencies since they have photovoltaic (PV) panels, which turn sunshine into electricity.

- **Lights Run on Solar Power:** Streetlights, garden

walkways, and outdoor lighting are all made with solar power. These solar-powered devices reduce electricity consumption and improve security by storing solar energy during the day and turning on automatically at night.

- **Solar Power Plants:** For travel, recreational vehicles, and emergency backup power, solar generators offer a portable power source. They provide a silent and clean substitute for conventional gas generators and are made out of solar panels, an inverter, and a battery storage system.

- **Water Heaters By Sunlight:** Utilizing solar panels, solar water heaters generate thermal energy from sunlight for use in heating water for residential or commercial use. Both energy costs and dependency on fossil fuels are greatly decreased by these solutions.

- **Solar Energy Systems for Homes:** Solar paneling, inverters, and battery storage are all part of complete house solar energy systems. A complete house can be powered by these devices, which lessens or even eliminates reliance on the grid. These systems are now more economical and effective because of technological advancements.

3.2 Devices for Wind Power

Wind power devices provide a sustainable and renewable power source by harnessing wind energy to generate electricity. These gadgets can be used in small-scale settings or in larger installations that have the capacity to generate substantial power.

- **Small Wind Generators:** Small-scale wind energy installations intended for domestic usage are known as micro wind turbines. They can be put in backyards or on rooftops to provide extra power and lower electricity costs. These wind turbines are perfect for locations with regular wind patterns.

- **Transportable Wind Turbines:** Because they are lightweight and portable, portable wind generators are a great option for outdoor enthusiasts and rural areas. These gadgets provide a dependable off-grid power option by being able to power tiny electrical devices and charge batteries.

- **Electrical Appliances:** Certain home gadgets are made expressly to run on wind energy. Examples of these are ventilation systems and water pumps that run on wind energy instead of traditional electricity.

- **Wind turbines with a vertical axis:** VAWTs are intended for urban settings with potentially constrained space and wind conditions. These wind turbines are appropriate for both residential and business settings since they are less noisy and intrusive than conventional horizontal axis wind turbines.

- **Systems Hybrid:** With hybrid systems, you can get a more steady and dependable energy supply by combining solar and wind power. These systems, which provide a constant power supply, are especially helpful in locations where one energy source may be less dependable.

3.3 Alternatives for Energy Storage

Solutions for energy storage are essential for controlling and maximizing the usage of renewable energy. Even with intermittent renewable energy sources, a steady and dependable power supply is guaranteed by environmentally friendly batteries and cutting-edge storage technology.

- **Batteries with Lithium Ion:** Because of its high energy density, extended longevity, and efficiency, lithium-ion batteries are frequently utilized for energy storage. These batteries offer dependable and sustainable energy storage and are utilized in solar power systems, electric cars, and portable electronics.

- **Batteries with Solid State:** A safer and more effective substitute for conventional lithium-ion batteries are solid-state batteries. By using solid electrolytes rather than liquid ones, they increase energy density and lower the possibility of leaks. For use in future renewable energy applications, these batteries show promise.

- **Flow Batteries:** Large-scale energy storage applications are a perfect fit for flow batteries. Utilizing liquid electrolytes that circulate through a stack of cells, they offer long-lasting and scalable energy storage. Grid storage and integration of renewable energy sources are appropriate uses for these batteries.

- **Air Energy Storage by Compressed Air:** By compressing air and storing it in subterranean caves, CAES systems store energy. Compressed air is released to power turbines and produce electricity as needed. Large-scale energy storage with little effect on the environment is made possible by this technique.

- **Storage of Flywheel Energy:** Flywheel systems use fast-spinning rotors to store energy. When required, the kinetic energy is transformed back into electrical energy. Flywheel storage is appropriate for grid stabilization and the integration of renewable energy sources since it is robust and efficient.

3.4 Integration of Smart Grids

In order to maximize energy consumption and improve grid efficiency, smart grids are necessary. Smart grid integration relies heavily on sustainable devices to maintain a stable and well-balanced energy system.

- **Smart Meters:** With the help of real-time data on energy use provided by smart meters, users can keep an eye on and control their energy usage. By lowering peak demand and optimizing energy distribution, these gadgets help utilities improve grid stability.

- **Demand reaction Systems:** In reaction to grid conditions, demand response systems modify energy use. These systems balance supply and demand and avoid grid overloads by using smart appliances and gadgets to shift or decrease energy use during peak hours.

- **Grid-Tied Inverters:** These devices transform DC electricity produced by wind turbines or solar panels into AC power that may be fed into the grid or utilized by home appliances. These inverters guarantee smooth grid integration and effective energy conversion.

- **Energy Management Systems:** To improve energy use in residences and commercial buildings, energy management systems (EMS) employ cutting-edge hardware and software. To provide effective and sustainable energy management, these systems incorporate smart devices, storage options, and renewable energy sources.

- The technology known as **Vehicle-to-Grid (V2G)** enables electric cars (EVs) to recycle energy back into the grid. By supplying extra energy storage and balancing supply and demand, particularly during peak hours, this technology promotes grid stability.

- **Dispersed Energy Resources (DERs):** Systems such as solar panels, wind turbines, and battery storage are examples of small-scale renewable energy resources, or DERs. By integrating these resources into the system, transmission losses are decreased and grid dependability is increased by providing decentralized and resilient energy solutions.

Investigating solar and wind power equipment, energy storage options, and how they integrate into smart grids are all necessary to comprehend renewable energy gadgets. Together, these technologies lessen the need for fossil fuels and have a smaller negative impact on the environment, paving the way for a robust and sustainable energy future.

CHAPTER 4

ECO-FRIENDLY TRANSPORTATION: ELECTRIC CARS AND BEYOND

4.1 The Revolution of Electric Vehicles

Due to the necessity of lowering carbon emissions and reducing reliance on fossil fuels, the automotive industry is witnessing a dramatic transition with the rise of electric cars (EVs). The characteristics of this revolution include growing consumer acceptance, government regulations that are favorable, and technological breakthroughs.

- **Technological Developments:** The range, efficiency, and affordability of electric vehicles (EVs) have been greatly enhanced by developments in battery technology, notably with regard to lithium-ion batteries. The efficiency and dependability of electric vehicles have also been improved by advancements in power electronics and electric drivetrains.

- **Received by Customers:** Consumers are becoming more receptive to adopting electric vehicles (EVs) as environmental issues gain consciousness. When compared to conventional internal combustion engine (ICE) vehicles, the overall cost of ownership for electric vehicles (EVs) which includes fuel and maintenance savings is becoming more attractive.

- **Policies of Governance:** Numerous governments are putting laws into place to promote the adoption of EVs. Along with non-financial benefits like lower registration costs, access to high-occupancy vehicle (HOV) lanes, and exemptions from some taxes, these also include financial incentives like tax credits, rebates, and grants.

- **Impact on the Environment:** Comparing EVs to ICE cars, EVs have zero tailpipe emissions, which dramatically lowers greenhouse gas emissions and air pollution. Both environmental sustainability and public health are enhanced by this.

- **Market Expansion:** With rising sales and a growing selection of models offered by leading automakers, the worldwide EV market is expanding quickly. Increased production capabilities and investments in R&D help to sustain this growth.

4.2 Infrastructure for Electric Vehicles

For EVs to be widely used, infrastructure for charging them must be developed. By guaranteeing EV customers have easy and dependable access to power, a strong and easily navigable network of charging stations lessens range anxiety and increases the utility of electric vehicles.

- **Points of Charge:** Public charging stations are being erected in a number of sites, such as residential complexes, workplaces, roads, and urban areas. To meet a range of needs, these stations offer three different charging levels: slow (Level 1), quick (Level 3), and in between.

- **Charging at Home:** The ease of home charging is a preference for many EV owners. The ability to install a home charging station guarantees that the car is prepared for usage every day by enabling overnight charge. Home charger installation is frequently aided by utility and government programs.

- **Fast Charging Networks**: By offering high-speed charging along main travel routes, fast charging networks, like Tesla's Supercharger network, facilitate long-distance travel. Long excursions become more viable thanks to these networks' considerable reduction in charging times.

- **Charging Wirelessly:** Modern plug-in chargers can be replaced with more practical and user-friendly wireless charging options thanks to emerging technologies. These devices streamline the charging process by transferring energy between a car and a charging station via electromagnetic fields.

- **Smart Charging:** By modifying power in response to grid situations, energy pricing, and user preferences, smart charging systems maximize the charging process. To further lessen the carbon imprint, these systems can also be integrated with renewable energy sources, such solar panels.

4.3 Vehicles Using Alternative Fuels

Although electric vehicles represent the vanguard of environmentally friendly transportation, other alternative fuel vehicles also help cut down on carbon emissions and the need for fossil fuels. These cars run on biofuels, hydrogen, and other renewable energy sources.

- **Fuel Cell Vehicles (FCVs) using Hydrogen:** Hydrogen is used in fuel cell vehicles (FCVs) to produce electricity by reacting chemically with oxygen; the only waste produced is water vapor. Similar to conventional vehicles, these vehicles have a high range and quick refilling times, which makes them a viable substitute for heavy-duty and long-distance applications.

- **Automotive Fuels:** Biofuels are made from renewable organic resources like garbage and plants, such as ethanol and biodiesel. Biofuel-powered vehicles emit fewer emissions than fossil fuel-powered ones, and they can frequently be employed in ICE vehicles already in production with only little modifications.

- **Vehicles that run on compressed natural gas (CNG):** Natural gas, which emits fewer emissions than either gasoline or diesel, is the fuel used in CNG cars. Natural gas is plentiful and provides a cleaner alternative when switching to fully renewable energy sources, even though it is not totally renewable.

- **Automotive Hybrids:** An internal combustion engine, an electric motor, and a battery are all combined in hybrid cars. When compared to conventional ICE vehicles, they provide better fuel economy and lower pollutants. By having the ability to be charged externally, plug-in hybrid electric vehicles (PHEVs) lessen their dependence on fossil fuels.

- **Flex-fuel and Ethanol Vehicles:** Flex-fuel cars offer flexibility and lower emissions by running on a blend of gasoline and ethanol. Usually made from corn or sugarcane, ethanol offers a sustainable substitute for fuels derived from petroleum.

4.4 Micro Mobility and Shared Mobility

Urban transportation is changing as a result of shared mobility and micro mobility services, which provide effective and sustainable substitutes for private vehicle ownership. These services create a more sustainable urban environment, cut emissions, and decrease the number of vehicles on the road.

- **Car-Sharing Services:** Users can borrow cars as needed through car-sharing programs, which eliminates the requirement for private vehicle ownership. By providing flexible and reasonably priced vehicle access, these services like Zipcar and Car2Go help to reduce the overall number of cars on the road.

- **Ride-Hailing Services:** By offering convenient transportation options, ride-hailing services such as Uber and Lyft lessen the demand for own automobiles. These services, especially when paired with electric and hybrid vehicles, can lower pollution and traffic congestion.

- **Programs for Bike Sharing:** For quick travels, bike-sharing programs provide a healthy and environmentally friendly mode of transportation. These initiatives, which are offered in numerous locations across the globe, make bicycles easily accessible, which lessens the need for motorized transportation and cuts emissions.

- **E-bikes and electric scooters**: Convenient and environmentally responsible options for urban mobility are e-scooters and e-bikes. With their ability to reduce dependency on cars and public transportation, these micro mobility solutions are perfect for short trips and last-mile connectivity.

- **Transportation Integration:** The efficiency and

convenience of urban transportation are increased when shared mobility services are integrated with public transit networks. This strategy provides continuous connectivity, which lowers emissions, improves public transportation utilization, and lessens traffic.

- **Urban Sustainability:** Sustainable urban design techniques that give priority to bicycling, walking, and public transportation are being adopted by cities more and more. These initiatives, which support the development of more sustainable and livable urban environments, include the construction of pedestrian-friendly zones, bike lanes, and effective public transportation systems.

Examining the electric vehicle revolution, the growth of EV infrastructure, alternative fuel cars, the function of shared mobility and micro mobility services, and other related topics are necessary to comprehend sustainable mobility. All of these factors work together to lower carbon emissions, improve urban sustainability, and encourage the development of a more efficient and clean transportation system in the future.

CHAPTER 5

Smart Living and GreenHouses

5.1 Eco-Friendly Household Appliances

Eco-friendly household appliances are essential for cutting down on energy use and protecting the environment. These appliances provide eco-friendly features and energy-efficient technologies that help households cut back on their carbon footprint and utility costs.

- **Refrigerators with Low Energy Use:** In order to use less energy, modern refrigerators are built with sophisticated temperature control systems, powerful compressors, and better insulation. For example, refrigerators with an Energy Star rating consume 10–50% less energy than regular ones, which considerably reduces the amount of electricity used in homes.

- **Shaving Equipment:** Over time, energy-efficient washing machines can result in significant savings because they consume less water and energy per load. In comparison to top-loading versions, front-loading washers are particularly renowned for their efficiency, consuming up to 40% less water and 50% less electricity. Efficiency is further increased by features like changeable water levels and load detection.

- **Sinks:** To consume less water and energy, modern dishwashers come equipped with technologies like heat pumps, effective water jets, and soil sensors. When compared to previous models, energy-efficient dishwashers can save over 5,000 gallons of water and reduce energy use by over 40% annually.

- **Intelligent Thermostats:** Nest and Ecobee are examples of smart thermostats that optimize heating and cooling schedules based on occupancy patterns and user preferences. These gadgets can cut HVAC energy consumption by up to 15% by analyzing usage patterns and automatically altering temperatures. This lowers energy costs and lowers carbon emissions.

- **Cooktop Induction Systems:** Traditional gas or electric stoves use less energy than induction cooktops. They shorten cooking times and energy loss by directly heating cookware using electromagnetic fields. Additionally, induction cooktops provide accurate temperature control and are safer.

5.2 Technology for Smart Homes

Utilizing artificial intelligence (AI) and the Internet of Things (IoT), smart home technology makes homes more pleasant, eco-friendly, and efficient. These innovations facilitate sustainable living, improve convenience, and maximize energy utilization.

- **Systems for Home Automation:** All-inclusive home automation systems, like those made by Control4 or Crestron, combine a variety of smart devices into a seamless network. These systems optimize energy use and improve convenience by enabling homeowners to operate lighting, heating, cooling, security, and entertainment systems from a single interface.

- **Smart Lighting:** Users can automate and manage lighting according to occupancy, time of day, and natural light levels with smart lighting systems like Philips Hue and LIFX. With these systems, you can save up to 40% on energy costs because lights are only turned on when necessary. Energy efficiency and user comfort are further improved by features including motion sensing, color temperature change, and dimming.

- **Energy Management Systems:** These systems keep an eye on and maximize the amount of energy used in homes. Real-time energy usage insights are provided by products such as Sense and Wiser Energy, which assist homes in identifying energy wasters and putting efficiency measures in place. Energy-saving automated activities, such shutting off unused gadgets or altering HVAC settings, are made possible by integration with smart home systems.

- **Conserving Water:** Rachio and Flo by Moen are two examples of smart water management systems that track water use, look for leaks, and set irrigation schedules automatically based on meteorological information. Especially in areas that are vulnerable to drought, these devices aid in minimizing water waste and encouraging sustainable water use.

- **Integrated Renewable Energy:** Wind turbines and solar panels are examples of renewable energy sources that smart home systems may interface with. Energy management systems minimize dependency on the grid, maximize the use of renewable energy sources, and store extra power in household batteries. This integration lessens its impact on the environment while improving energy independence.

5.3 Eco-Friendly Building Supplies

Choosing environmentally friendly building materials is crucial to designing environmentally responsible homes.

These materials support healthier indoor conditions, improve energy efficiency, and use less resources.

- **Materials Reclaimed & Recycled:** Utilizing recovered and repurposed materials decreases waste and lowers the need for new resources. Reclaimed wood, recycled metal, and repurposed bricks are a few examples. These materials give homes a distinctive character while also conserving resources.

- **Sustainable Wood Products:** Forests that are properly managed provide the wood for certified sustainable products, like those with the Forest Stewardship Council (FSC) mark. These goods contribute to lessening deforestation and preserving ecosystems. Cross-laminated timber (CLT) and other engineered wood products provide durable, environmentally friendly substitutes for conventional building materials.

- **Insulation Materials:** Recycled denim, cellulose, and sheep's wool are a few examples of eco-friendly insulation materials that offer superior thermal performance with little negative environmental impact. These materials lower energy usage, enhance indoor air quality, and are non-toxic.

- **Low-VOC Finishes and Paints:** Traditional paints and finishes include volatile organic compounds (VOCs), which are linked to indoor air pollution and health issues. Low- and zero-VOC substitutes lessen dangerous emissions, enhancing indoor air quality and fostering healthier living environments.

- **Energy-Efficient Windows:** High-performance windows greatly improve a home's energy efficiency. Examples of these are double or triple glazing, low-emissivity (low-E) coatings, and gas fills. These windows improve comfort and cut energy costs by reducing heat gain in the summer and loss of heat in the winter.

- **Excellent Roofs:** In order to minimize heat absorption, lower cooling expenses, and lessen the impact of the urban heat island, cool roofs employ reflecting materials. Significant energy savings can be achieved by reducing roof temperatures by up to 50°F with materials including cool shingles, tiles, and reflecting coatings.

5.4 The Health and Quality of Indoor Air

For optimal health and wellbeing, indoor air quality (IAQ) must be maintained. By lowering allergens, pollutants, and humidity levels, IAQ-improving devices and technologies contribute to the creation of healthier living spaces.

- **Air Purifiers:** HEPA-filtered air purifiers, like those made by Dyson and Blueair, remove smoke, pollen, dust, and pet dander from the air. In order to improve overall air quality, certain models further come with activated carbon filters to eliminate smells and volatile organic compounds (VOCs).

- **Air Conditioning Systems:** Having adequate ventilation is crucial to having a healthy IAQ. In order to improve efficiency and comfort, energy recovery ventilators (ERVs) and heat recovery ventilators (HRVs) collect energy from exhaust air while supplying new air. These systems aid in controlling humidity levels and lowering indoor pollution.

- **Intelligent Air Quality Thermostats:** Temperature, humidity, and CO_2 levels are just a few of the air quality characteristics that smart thermostats with built-in IAQ sensors monitor and manage. In order to maintain the ideal IAQ and improve comfort and health, these devices have the ability to automatically modify filtration and ventilation systems.

- **Control Humidity:** IAQ requires maintaining ideal humidity levels (30–50%). Reducing the chance of mold formation and respiratory issues is possible by controlling indoor humidity with the use of dehumidifiers and humidifiers, including those made by Honeywell and Aprilaire.

- **Verdant flora:** Through the release of oxygen and absorption of CO_2, indoor plants can naturally improve IAQ. A healthy interior atmosphere is enhanced by certain plants, such as peace lilies, spider plants, and snake plants, which also eliminate pollutants from the air.

- **Digital Home Helpers:** IAQ monitors and smart home systems can be integrated with devices such as Amazon Echo and Google Home to offer real-time updates and control over air quality. With the voice-activated ease that these assistants provide, managing and keeping an eye on IAQ is simple.

Important first steps in developing green houses and encouraging smart living include integrating sustainable home appliances, smart home technology, green building materials, and indoor air quality enhancements. These actions contribute to a more sustainable future by improving comfort, health, and well-being in addition to lessening the impact on the environment.

CHAPTER 6

WEARABLE TECHNOLOGY AND FASHION WITH A CONSCIENCE

6.1 Eco-Friendly Fashion Technology

The fashion industry is changing dramatically as it incorporates more environmentally friendly procedures and technology. To minimize waste and lessen the environmental impact of the fashion industry, sustainable fashion tech emphasizes the use of eco-friendly materials, the implementation of environmentally conscious production techniques, and the promotion of recycling programs.

- **Sustainable Materials:** Sustainable fashion is leading the way in the usage of environmentally friendly materials. Textiles that are biodegradable, renewable, and require fewer resources are being made with a greater emphasis on organic cotton, hemp, bamboo, and recycled fibers. These materials lessen reliance on synthetic fibers, which come from petroleum and add to the pollution caused by microplastics, and traditional cotton, which uses a lot of water and pesticides.

- **Innovative Fabrics:** Piñatex (made from pineapple leaf fibers), Tencel (produced from wood pulp sourced responsibly), and Econyl (regenerated nylon from ocean and landfill debris) are examples of innovative fabrics developed as a result of advances in material science. These textiles provide great performance and visual appeal as sustainable substitutes for traditional materials.

- **Eco-Friendly Dyeing and Finishing Techniques:** The garment industry's traditional dyeing and finishing techniques are infamous for being very water-intensive and environmentally harmful. Eco-friendly substitutes that use less water and chemicals include digital printing, waterless dyeing, and natural dyes made from plants and minerals. By reducing their negative effects on the environment, technologies like AirDye and ColorZen are reinventing textile dyeing.

- **Recycling Projects:** Recycling programs are being embraced by fashion firms more frequently in an effort to complete the cycle of fashion. Take-back programs, in which customers recycle their unwanted apparel, and the incorporation of recycled materials into new collections are examples of programs that are becoming more and more popular. Leading the way in recycling and circular fashion are companies like Patagonia and H&M.

- **Sustainable Production Processes:** Using ecologically friendly production methods is another aspect of sustainable fashion technology. Low-impact manufacturing methods reduce material waste and energy usage. Examples include 3D knitting, laser cutting, and zero-waste pattern making. Furthermore, local manufacturing and on-demand production lessen the carbon footprint brought on by transportation and surplus inventories.

6.2 Wise Accessories

The health and convenience benefits of smart wearables, including fitness trackers and smartwatches, are driving up their popularity. But it's important to think about how these gadgets affect the environment and look into ways to make them more sustainable.

- **Smart Wearables Benefits**: Numerous advantages come with smart wearables, such as connectivity, fitness tracking, and health monitoring. Users may make educated decisions about their health with the help of gadgets like the Apple Watch and Fitbit, which offer real-time data on heart rate, activity levels, sleep patterns, and more. With the help of social sharing capabilities, goal-setting tools, and reminders, these gadgets also encourage exercise and overall wellbeing.

- **Impact on the Environment:** Smart wearable manufacturing and disposal add to resource depletion and electronic trash (e-waste). These devices' use of plastics, batteries, and rare earth metals raises questions about their environmental impact. Wearables and other e-waste from abandoned electronics present major recycling and waste management problems.

- **Eco-friendly Architecture and Materials**: Sustainable design and material solutions are being investigated by manufacturers to reduce the environmental impact of smart wearables. Resource consumption and waste can be decreased by using recycled and biodegradable materials, such as eco-friendly fabrics, bio-based polymers, and reclaimed metal. Wearables have longer lifespans when they have modular designs that make component replacement and repair simple.

- **Efficiency of Energy:** Reducing the environmental impact of smart wearables requires improving their energy efficiency. Advances in battery technology, including wearables that run on solar power or capture kinetic energy, can lessen the need for frequent charging and dependency on non-renewable energy sources. Sustainability is further improved via low-energy communication protocols like Bluetooth Low Energy (BLE) and effective power management systems.

6.3 Augmented and Virtual Reality

By lessening the fashion industry's environmental impact, virtual and augmented reality (VR/AR) technologies have the potential to completely transform the sector. With the help of these technologies, fashion can be designed, presented, and experienced in new and creative ways that use less material resources and produce less waste.

- **Online Fashion Exhibitions:** VR/AR-enabled virtual fashion shows offer a more environmentally friendly option than conventional runway presentations. Designers may present their collections to a worldwide audience without the need for real locations, travel, or overly produced content by building immersive virtual environments. This encourages accessibility and lessens the carbon footprint connected to fashion events.

- **Digital Demos:** Customers may virtually try on apparel and accessories without having to physically try them on thanks to technology. As a result, there is less need for shipping and returns, which in the fashion business are major sources of waste and carbon emissions. Virtual fitting rooms and augmented reality fashion mirrors are two examples of apps that improve online shopping and promote smarter purchasing choices.

- **Virtual Style:** Digital fashion is becoming more and more popular, involving clothes and accessories that are only available online. Virtual clothing designers make clothing that can be worn in virtual worlds, games, and social media. This minimizes textile waste and does away with the requirement for physical production. Additionally, digital fashion creates new platforms for self-expression and innovation.

- **Sustainable Design Processes:** Virtual reality and augmented reality technologies reduce the need for physical samples and iterations by enabling designers to create and test prototypes virtually. This reduces material waste, speeds up the design process, and encourages more environmentally friendly behaviors. The way fashion is conceived and developed is changing because of digital design tools like CLO3D and Browzwear.

6.4 Transparent and Ethical Supply Chains

In the fashion and wearable technology industries, ethical and transparent supply chains are critical to advancing fair labor practices and sustainability. Maintaining accountability and traceability across the whole supply chain contributes to the defense of workers' rights and the mitigation of environmental damage.

- **Equitable Work Practices:** Fair labor practices are given top priority in ethical supply chains, guaranteeing that employees receive just compensation, work in safe environments, and have access to fundamental rights and benefits. Companies that uphold the labor standards established by Fair Trade and the Ethical Trading Initiative, among other organizations, certify factories and suppliers with whom they work.

- **Transparency and Traceability:** Supply chain transparency enables customers to follow a product's journey from raw ingredients to finished goods. Consumers are more likely to trust and support brands that provide details about their supply chain, including sourcing, production, and labor methods. The application of blockchain technology to improve traceability and confirm the legitimacy of sustainable practices is growing.

- **Sustainable procurement:** Sustainable raw material procurement is given priority in ethical supply chains. This includes conserving the environment, promoting biodiversity, and employing organic and renewable resources. The ethical sourcing of materials is guaranteed by certifications such as the Forest Stewardship Council (FSC) and the Global Organic Textile Standard (GOTS).

- **Reduction of Waste and Circularity:** Cutting waste and promoting circular fashion are essential components of ethical supply chains. Companies are putting into practice programs like upcycling, clothes recycling, and designing with longevity and repairability in mind. These methods preserve resources, prolong the life of products, and cut down on waste going to landfills.

- **Awareness and Advocacy of Consumers:** Making educated decisions regarding purchases is encouraged when customers are aware of the value of ethical and sustainable design. Companies can launch advocacy and awareness efforts to draw attention to the consequences of their actions and persuade customers to embrace supply chains that are honest and transparent.

The wearable technology and fashion sectors are leading the way in sustainable and moral business practices. Through the implementation of sustainable materials, inventive production techniques, intelligent technology, and open supply chains, these industries are leading the path towards a future that is both environmentally sensitive and sustainable.

CHAPTER 7

Eco-Friendly Entertainment and Gaming

7.1 Sustainable Game Consoles and Add-ons

The game business, which is well-known for its quick technological progress and immense appeal, is becoming more and more aware of how important sustainability is. This movement is led by eco-friendly gaming consoles and accessories, which emphasize energy economy and the use of sustainable materials to lessen their negative effects on the environment.

- **Game Hardware with Low Energy Consumption**: Energy efficiency is a consideration in the design of modern gaming consoles. Power-saving settings, energy-efficient processors, and cooling solutions that don't sacrifice performance are being added by manufacturers. Consoles such as the PlayStation 5 and Xbox Series X, for instance, include low-power standby modes that drastically cut down on energy usage while the device is not in use.

- **Earth-friendly Materials:** A lot of plastic, metal, and other elements that can have a big environmental impact are used in the manufacturing of gaming consoles and peripherals. Businesses are using sustainable materials like biodegradable parts, recycled plastics, and ethically sourced metals to address this. Innovative materials like bioplastics, which are made from renewable resources and have comparable performance qualities to conventional plastics but a smaller environmental impact, are also being investigated by some businesses.

- **Management of E-Waste and Recycling**: Electronic garbage, or "e-waste," is another issue that the game industry is tackling. Recycle programs for old consoles and accessories: Major brands are enticing customers to return their outdated electronics for appropriate disposal and recycling. These initiatives lessen the quantity of e-waste that ends up in landfills and aid in the recovery of valuable materials. Businesses such as Microsoft, Sony, and Nintendo have implemented recycling and take-back programs to guarantee that products at the end of their useful life are disposed of properly.

7.2 Virtual Environments and Teacher Education

With its ability to create immersive experiences that increase awareness and support conservation efforts, virtual reality (VR) technology has the potential to completely transform environmental education. Users can interact with and learn about environmental challenges in a memorable and meaningful way with virtual reality.

- **Environmental Immersion Experiences:** Through virtual reality (VR), users can travel to different regions of the world, experiencing a variety of ecosystems and directly witnessing the effects of environmental degradation. VR experiences, for instance, can replicate the effects of plastic pollution in the ocean, the melting of the polar ice caps, and the destruction of rainforests. These immersive learning environments encourage a sense of urgency in addressing environmental concerns by giving users a greater grasp of them.

- **Academic Initiatives:** VR is being used by educational institutions and environmental organizations to develop captivating curricula. These educational resources can be used to teach people about biodiversity, climate change, and sustainable behaviors in public awareness campaigns, classrooms, and museums. Professionals in disciplines like environmental management and conservation can benefit from VR training as well, as it offers lifelike simulations of a range of situations and difficulties.

- **Active Education:** Virtual reality provides engaging learning experiences that surpass conventional teaching approaches. Users can actively engage in environmental acts by taking part in virtual clean-up drives, reforestation projects, or wildlife conservation efforts. This practical method improves learning and promotes constructive behavioral adjustments.

7.3 Eco-Friendly Gaming Methods

Adopting routines and environments that lower energy usage, support recycling, and promote responsible gaming are all part of sustainable gaming practices. A more sustainable gaming environment is something that manufacturers, developers, and players can all contribute to.

- **Settings to Save Energy:** Numerous PCs and game consoles have energy-saving options that can drastically cut down on power usage. Gamers can reduce their environmental effect by utilizing features like energy-efficient display settings, low-power standby modes, and automated shutdown. Gamers can also maximize the energy economy of their devices by modifying the brightness settings, turning off unused functions, and making sure their systems have adequate ventilation to avoid overheating.

- **Programs for Recycling:** Programs for recycling

gaming accessories and hardware are crucial for controlling e-waste. Gamers can make sure their outdated devices are disposed of and recycled correctly by taking part in municipal e-waste recycling initiatives or manufacturer take-back programs. Furthermore, you may prolong the life of functional equipment and cut down on waste by selling or donating them.

- **Conscious Gaming Practices:** In addition to controlling energy use, responsible gaming practices promote a positive balance between gaming and other activities. Gamers who play video games too much may use more energy and experience health problems. It is advised of gamers to take regular pauses, move their bodies, and lead balanced lives. Further cutting waste is possible by doing away with the requirement for actual game discs and packaging with the help of digital downloads and cloud gaming services.

7.4 Sustainable Entertainment's Future

The development and uptake of new trends and technologies that put environmental responsibility first will determine the direction of sustainable entertainment in the future. There are a number of important areas where sustainable practices are likely to have a big impact as the sector develops.

- **Cloud Gaming:** Gamers no longer require powerful local gear because cloud gaming services like Google Stadia, Xbox Cloud Gaming, and NVIDIA GeForce Now enable them to stream games straight from data centers. Cloud gaming can lower electronic waste and increase energy efficiency by centralizing computing resources. To optimize sustainability, it's crucial to make sure data centers are fueled by renewable energy sources.

- **Creating Sustainable Content:** The incorporation of sustainability themes and educational information into video games is becoming more common among game makers. Players' attitudes and behaviors can be influenced by games that encourage conservation, environmental awareness, and sustainable practices. In addition, developers are implementing environmentally responsible development techniques, like limiting the carbon impact of game production and employing renewable energy in studios.

- **Online Performances and Events:** The popularity of online performances and events provides a long-term substitute for conventional live events. Large-scale virtual concerts and festivals have been held on virtual platforms like Roblox, Fortnite, and VRChat, which has lessened the environmental effect of travel, venue construction, and garbage production. Additionally, these virtual events are globally accessible, so that more individuals can take part without having to be present in person.

- **NFTs and Blockchain:** Non-fungible tokens (NFTs) and blockchain technology have the power to completely transform digital ownership and transactions in the entertainment sector. The environmental effects of blockchain activities, in particular the high energy usage of some blockchain networks, must be addressed. Proof-of-stake (PoS) techniques, among other innovations in energy-efficient blockchain technologies, can help allay these worries.

Eco-friendly hardware, immersive environmental education, sustainable gaming practices, and upcoming technologies are all helping the gaming and entertainment industries get closer to sustainability. These industries may maintain their innovation while lessening their environmental impact and fostering a more sustainable future by placing a high priority on environmental responsibility.

CHAPTER 8

GREEN TECHNOLOGY MARKET CHALLENGES AND OPPORTUNITIES

8.1 Adoption and Perception by Consumers

Consumer adoption of green technology goods is impacted by a number of variables, such as availability, cost, perceived benefits, and awareness. Comprehending these variables is imperative for enterprises and legislators seeking to propel the market for environmentally friendly solutions.

Education and Awareness:

1. A lot of customers are still ignorant of the advantages and accessibility of green technology items. Public education campaigns regarding the benefits of these technologies for the economy and environment are crucial.

2. Adopting green technology can result in long-term

cost savings, health advantages, and good environmental effects. These points should be emphasized in educational campaigns and marketing initiatives.

Perceived Benefits and Efficacy:

1. Green tech products must be shown effectively in the eyes of consumers. Putting on display dependable functionality, robustness, and ease of use might help dispel doubts.

2. Building trust and confidence can be facilitated via case studies, evaluations, and testimonials that highlight successful adoption of green technology products.

Price and Accessibility:

1. The initial expense of green technology is one of the main obstacles to its acceptance. Many customers believe that sustainable items are more costly than their traditional counterparts. Making green technology more affordable through subsidies, flexible payment plans, and financial incentives can help it become more widely available.

Accessibility and Availability:

1. The adoption of green technology goods may be impeded by restricted channels of distribution and availability. Accessibility can be enhanced via growing online markets and retail networks.

2. Increasing the reach of green tech products through partnerships with distributors and retailers can contribute to their mainstreaming.

8.2 Policies and Incentives of the Government

The adoption and development of green technology are greatly aided by government policies and incentives. A well-designed legislative framework can stimulate innovation, cut expenses, and quicken the expansion of the market.

Regulatory Frameworks:

1. Lawmakers have the authority to enact guidelines and standards requiring the application of green technologies across a range of industries. For instance, fuel efficiency requirements for

automobiles may be determined by legislation, and building rules may mandate energy-efficient construction methods.

2. Putting in place carbon pricing tools, such cap-and-trade or carbon taxes, can encourage companies to use cleaner technology and cut emissions.

Financial Incentives:

1. Grants, tax credits, and subsidies can reduce the cost barriers for companies and consumers to invest in green technology. Sustainable products may become more appealing and cheap as a result of these incentives.

2. Low-interest loans and government-backed funding schemes can help small and medium-sized businesses (SMEs) develop and implement green technologies.

Support for Research and Development:

1. Innovation in the green tech industry can be stimulated by public support for research and development (R&D). The development of new

technologies and the investigation of current ones can be aided by grants and financing initiatives.

2. Partnerships between public and private organizations, as well as academia, can promote information exchange and quicken the development of new technologies.

Public Awareness initiatives:

1. To inform the public about the advantages of green technologies and promote sustainable practices, governments might spearhead public awareness initiatives.

2. Collaborations between media outlets, community organizations, and non-governmental organizations (NGOs) can increase the campaigns' impact and reach.

8.3 Sustainability of the Supply Chain

In the green tech industry, creating supply chains that are both morally and ecologically sound presents a big challenge. Keeping the supply chain sustainable can improve the effect and reputation of green technology goods.

Ethical Sourcing:

1. Businesses must make sure that raw materials are supplied ethically, without harming the environment or infringing on human rights. Using recyclable, renewable, or sustainably sourced materials is part of this. Verifying the ethical sourcing of commodities can be facilitated by establishing transparent supply chains with traceability tools. Consumers might be reassured by certifications and standards like Fair Trade and Forest Stewardship Council (FSC).

Green Manufacturing:

1. Sustainable manufacturing techniques reduce emissions, waste, and energy use in the course of production. This can be accomplished by using energy-efficient technologies and embracing the concepts of the circular economy.
2. To further lessen their carbon impact, manufacturers can power their operations using renewable energy sources like solar and wind.

Logistics and Transportation:

1. Supply chains' environmental effect can be considerably decreased by streamlining logistics and transportation. This entails utilizing fuel-efficient cars, planning delivery routes, and implementing low-emission modes of transportation.

2. In order to cut emissions by eliminating the need for long-distance transportation, businesses can also look into local sourcing and production.

Management of Waste and Recycling:

1. Sustainable supply networks require effective waste management techniques. Companies can guarantee that goods and materials are reused or disposed of ethically by putting in place recycling programs and take-back initiatives.

2. Supply chains can be made more sustainable by designing items with end-of-life considerations, such as easy disassembly and recyclability.

8.4 New Developments in Technology and Upcoming Trends

Emerging trends and technology are reshaping the green tech market, which is always changing. Keeping up with these advancements is essential for companies and decision-makers who want to fully utilize sustainable solutions.

Advanced Renewable Energy Technologies:

1. The shift to clean energy is being fueled by advancements in renewable energy, including bioenergy solutions, advanced wind turbines, and next-generation solar panels. These technologies offer increased scalability, reduced costs, and increased efficiency.

2. The potential for generating renewable power is increasing with research into new energy sources including geothermal and tidal energy.

Smart Grids and Energy Storage:

1. To get around the intermittent nature of renewable energy sources, sophisticated energy storage

technologies like supercapacitors and solid-state batteries must be developed. More dependable and resilient energy systems may be made possible by advancements in storage technologies. Artificial intelligence (AI) and the Internet of Things (IoT) are two components of smart grid technologies that can optimize energy distribution, cut waste, and improve grid stability.

Food Technology and Sustainable Agriculture:

1. Technological advancements in sustainable agriculture, such lab-grown meat, vertical farming, and precision farming, are revolutionizing the food industry. These innovations seek to improve food security, decrease environmental effect, and use less resources.

2. The environmental issues connected to traditional agriculture and food processing are being addressed by advancements in food technology, such as plant-based proteins and sustainable packaging.

Recycled Materials and Waste Handling:

1. Reuse, recycling, and waste minimization are key

components of the circular economy model, which is gaining popularity. This shift is being aided by advances in materials science, such as the development of biodegradable plastics and sophisticated recycling methods.

2. The sustainability of waste management systems is being improved by technologies that provide effective resource recovery and waste-to-energy conversion.

Sustainable urban development and green building:

1. The future of urban development is being shaped by developments in green building technology, including sustainable materials, smart building systems, and energy-efficient construction techniques. The goal of these advances is to build more sustainable and healthier living spaces.

2. The idea of smart cities which combine sustainability and technology is what's motivating urban planning projects. The main goals of smart city solutions are to maximize resource use, lower emissions, and improve the standard of living for locals.

There are many opportunities and problems in the green tech industry. Encouraging the growth and effect of sustainable technology requires a grasp of customer views, utilizing government backing, maintaining a sustainable supply chain, and staying ahead of future innovations. Businesses and legislators may help create a more sustainable and prosperous future by tackling these factors.

CHAPTER 9

CASE STUDIES: PROMISING GREEN TECHNOLOGY BUSINESSES

9.1 Detailed Exam of Top Green Technology Businesses

Many businesses in the green technology space are leading the way in sustainability. This section offers insightful analysis and inspirational examples of numerous top companies that have effectively incorporated sustainable practices into their daily operations.

Model Tesla, Inc.:

1. With its high-performance electric vehicles, Tesla has revolutionized the market as a pioneer in the electric vehicle (EV) business. The company has distinguished itself as a leader in green technology by its emphasis on innovation and commitment to expediting the global shift to sustainable energy. - The creation of energy storage devices like the Powerwall and Powerpack, as well as the growth of

its solar energy division through SolarCity, are important projects.

Ørsted:

1. Ørsted, previously Danish Oil and Natural Gas (DONG), is today a world leader in renewable energy, having transitioned from an energy corporation reliant on fossil fuels. The business has made major investments in offshore wind farms, making it one of the biggest offshore wind energy producers. Ørsted has demonstrated its dedication to sustainability by aiming to become carbon neutral by 2025 and eliminating coal completely by 2023.

Extraordinary Meat:

1. A pioneer in the food innovation sector, Beyond Meat is well-known for its plant-based meat alternatives. Beyond Meat tackles environmental issues associated with cattle ranching, including greenhouse gas emissions, water use, and land degradation, by offering substitutes for animal protein. The company's success is ascribed to its emphasis on product development, which makes

sure that its plant-based products taste and feel much like traditional meat, appealing to a wide range of consumers.

Patagonia:

1. Known for its dedication to social and environmental responsibility, Patagonia is a pioneer in the sustainable fashion sector. The company supports fair labor standards across its supply chain and incorporates organic and recyclable materials into its goods.

2. Through programs like the Worn Wear program, Patagonia encourages customers to recycle and repair their apparel, cutting waste and advancing the circular economy.

9.2 Best Practices and Lessons Learned

1. Examining the tactics and procedures of prosperous green tech firms can teach other companies striving for sustainability a lot of useful lessons. Important lessons learned include:

Investment in R&D and Innovation:

1. Research & development expenditures must be sustained in order to foster innovation in green technology. Businesses such as Tesla and Beyond Meat have made significant investments in research and development to create innovative goods that satisfy consumer needs and advance sustainability.

2. Encouraging staff to experiment with new concepts and technologies boosts the organization's growth and competitive advantage.

Strong Mission and Vision:

1. A company's strategic decisions can be guided by a compelling mission, like Ørsted's shift to renewable energy, which can also motivate stakeholders. Bringing in environmentally concerned customers and fostering brand loyalty are two benefits of aligning business operations with a sustainable goal.

2. Strong missions help companies win over investors who are giving environmental, social, and governance (ESG) considerations more weight.

Consumer Engagement and Education:

1. Raising consumer awareness of the advantages of green technology goods is crucial to accelerating their uptake. Customers are educated about sustainable methods and gain trust from Patagonia's openness regarding its supply chain and environmental impact.

2. Establishing and maintaining long-term relationships with customers can be achieved by interacting with them on social media, through community activities, and through sustainability reports.

Sustainable Supply Chain Management:

1. It's imperative to guarantee sustainability all the way through the supply chain. Businesses can use techniques that reduce their influence on the environment, like using recycled materials, cutting back on energy use, and enforcing fair labor standards.

2. Supply chain integrity and resilience can be increased through collaborations with stakeholders and suppliers who share the company's commitment

to sustainability.

9.3 Developing Resilience and Overcoming Obstacles

Market rivalry and regulatory obstacles are only two of the many difficulties that prosperous green tech businesses frequently encounter. The secret to their long-term success is their capacity to overcome these setbacks and develop resilience.

Switching with the Market:

1. The green technology market is always changing due to shifting customer tastes and advances in technology. Businesses need to be flexible and nimble, constantly observing market developments and modifying their approaches as necessary.

2. As an example of its capacity to diversify and seize new possibilities, consider Tesla's entry into the energy storage and solar energy sectors.

Navigating Regulatory Environments:

1. Adherence to environmental laws and guidelines can be difficult and differ depending on the location. To

maintain compliance, businesses must keep up with changes in regulations and proactively modify their procedures.

2. Having conversations with legislators and taking part in business advocacy can help mold regulatory frameworks that are advantageous and promote the expansion of the green tech sector.

Financial Sustainability:

1. For green tech businesses, especially those in their infancy, obtaining capital and efficiently allocating financial resources are critical. Financial stability can be improved by effective resource management, strategic alliances, and investor interactions.

2. Government subsidies and incentives for environmentally friendly projects can offer extra funding, enabling businesses to expand and make investments in cutting-edge technology.

9.4 Creative Ingenuity

1. The green tech revolution is centered on innovation, which is fueled by an entrepreneurial spirit and

teamwork. Examining the function of innovation reveals the impact of group effort as well as the possibility for additional breakthroughs.

Startups and Entrepreneurship:

1. Innovation in green tech is largely driven by entrepreneurs. Startups frequently challenge old conventions and test the limits of sustainability by bringing novel viewpoints and innovative technologies to the market.

2. An active network of green tech entrepreneurs can be created by encouraging entrepreneurship through funding possibilities, incubators, and accelerators.

Partnerships and Collaboration:

1. Businesses, governments, academic institutions, and nonprofits can work together to develop and use sustainable technologies more quickly. Public-private partnerships and joint ventures make use of a variety of resources and areas of expertise.

2. Open innovation platforms and industry consortia are examples of initiatives that can help with information sharing and cooperative problem

solving.

Integration Across Industries:

1. The impact of green technology solutions can be increased by integrating them across different industries. One way to promote overall sustainability is through the use of renewable energy technology into industrial, transportation, and agriculture.

2. Cross-industry cooperation can also encourage the creation of novel business models and hybrid technologies that concurrently address several environmental issues.

Case studies of prosperous green technology businesses provide insightful information about the tactics, difficulties, and breakthroughs influencing the field of sustainable technology. Businesses may embrace best practices, develop resilience, and contribute to a greener future by taking note of these examples. The way the green tech industry is still developing emphasizes how crucial it is to maintain a dedication to sustainability, cooperation, and constant innovation.

CHAPTER 10

SUSTAINABLE TECHNOLOGY'S FUTURE: A GREENER TOMORROW

10.1 Green Technology's Effect on Society

The extensive use of environmentally friendly technology has the potential to have a profound effect on society in a number of ways. Green technology has advantages for the economy, society, and health in addition to environmental protection as it becomes more ingrained in daily life.

Environmental Advantages:

1. Decrease in greenhouse gas emissions: Using energy-efficient appliances, renewable energy sources, and electric cars all help to reduce carbon footprints.
2. Preserving the environment: Sustainable technology encourages the utilization of regenerative resources and lessens reliance on limited resources.
3. contamination reduction: Less contamination of the

air, water, and soil results from cleaner production methods and goods.

Economic Benefits:

1. Job creation: The green tech industry creates jobs in manufacturing, maintenance, research, and development.
2. Cost savings: Energy-efficient technology lowers operating expenses for enterprises and electricity bills for households.
3. Market expansion and investment are driven by the growing demand for sustainable products.

Social Advantages:

1. Better public health: Healthier living conditions are a result of lower pollution levels and improved indoor air quality.
2. Improved quality of life: Having access to renewable energy, environmentally friendly transportation, and smart home technology raises standards of living.
3. Greater education and awareness: The use of green technology encourages sustainable activities and increases public knowledge of environmental

challenges.

10.2 Technology's Contribution to Reaching Sustainable Development Goals

The Sustainable Development Goals (SDGs) of the United Nations are greatly advanced by green technology. Sustainable technology supports worldwide sustainability initiatives by tackling a range of environmental, economic, and social issues.

SDG 7: Accessible and Sustainable Energy:

1. Renewable energy technologies, like wind and solar power, increase access to electricity in isolated and underserved places by offering clean, inexpensive energy options.
2. Innovations in energy storage provide a dependable and effective energy source, facilitating the shift to a sustainable energy system.

SDG 11 - Sustainable Cities and Communities:

1. Resource efficiency, waste reduction, and enhanced urban living conditions are all achieved through

smart city technologies.

2. Energy-efficient appliances and environmentally friendly building materials support the creation of sustainable infrastructure.

SDG 12-Responsible Consumption and Production:

1. Circular economy ideas, such recycling and reuse, reduce waste and encourage environmentally friendly production methods.

2. Eco-friendly packaging and goods lessen their negative effects on the environment and promote sensible use.

SDG 13 - climate Action:

1. Green tech innovations increase resilience to climatic effects and reduce emissions, thereby mitigating climate change.

2. Predictive and monitoring technologies help address climate change in a proactive manner.

(SDGs) 14 and 15

1. Ecosystems and biodiversity are safeguarded by sustainable practices in forestry, agriculture, and

fisheries, as per Sustainable Development Goals (SDGs) 14 and 15.

2. Pollution control methods shield land and marine life from harm.

10.3 Initiation of Action

A brighter future demands the combined efforts of citizens, companies, and governments. One of the most important steps in building a more resilient and sustainable world is adopting sustainable technologies.

People:

1. Develop environmentally responsible behaviors: Make use of sustainable items, cut trash, and use energy-efficient appliances.

2. Encourage green tech businesses: Buy from companies who put an emphasis on sustainability and make investments in creative solutions.

3. Promote and instruct: Encourage the adoption of environmental legislation and spread knowledge about the advantages of green technology.

Companies:

1. Incorporate eco-friendly materials, minimize waste, and use energy-efficient procedures into daily operations to promote sustainability.

2. Innovate and Invest: Create and finance environmentally conscious technology solutions.

3. Work together and take the lead: Establish industry standards and promote sustainability by collaborating with other companies, NGOs, and governments.

Governments:

1. Put in place laws that are helpful: Encourage green tech innovation with grants, tax advantages, and subsidies.

2. Control and uphold: Enact and uphold laws that encourage sustainability and lessen their negative effects on the environment.

3. Inform and involve: To promote sustainable practices, organize public awareness campaigns and interact with relevant parties.

10.4 Recap

Sustainable technology has a bright future ahead of it, full with opportunity to positively impact the social, economic, and environmental domains. The substantial influence of green technology on society, its critical role in accomplishing the Sustainable Development Goals, and the group efforts necessary to promote a greener future have all been covered in this chapter.

Main Findings:

1. Green technology has several advantages, such as lower emissions, financial savings, the creation of jobs, and enhanced public health.

2. Achieving the Sustainable Development Goals (SDGs) and promoting global sustainability initiatives depend on sustainable technologies.

3. Governments, corporations, and individuals must work together to promote the invention and uptake of green technology.

The Course of Action:

1. Persistent innovation: To advance green tech solutions and meet new environmental concerns, ongoing research and development are essential.

2. Collaboration: The impact of sustainable technology will be amplified by successful cross-sector partnerships and collaborations.

3. Commitment: The successful integration of green technology into daily life will depend on the unwavering commitment to sustainability shown by all stakeholders.

The answer to a more robust and environmentally friendly future lies in the sustainable tech sector. We can create the foundation for a more promising and sustainable future by embracing innovation, encouraging teamwork, and demonstrating our commitment to sustainability.

ABOUT THE AUTHOR

 Author and thought leader in the IT field Taylor Royce is well known. He has a two-decade career and is an expert at tech trend analysis and forecasting, which enables a wide audience to understand complicated concepts.

Royce's considerable involvement in the IT industry stemmed from his passion with technology, which he developed during his computer science studies. He has extensive knowledge of the industry because of his experience in both software development and strategic consulting.

Known for his research and lucidity, he has written multiple best-selling books and contributed to esteemed tech periodicals. Translations of Royce's books throughout the world demonstrate his impact.

Royce is a well-known authority on emerging technologies and their effects on society, frequently requested as a speaker at international conferences and as a guest on tech podcasts. He promotes the development of ethical technology, emphasizing problems like data privacy and the digital divide.

In addition, with a focus on sustainable industry growth, Royce mentors upcoming tech experts and supports IT education projects. Taylor Royce is well known for his ability to combine analytical thinking with technical know-how. He sees a time when technology will ethically benefit humanity.

www.ingramcontent.com/pod-product-compliance
Lightning Source LLC
Chambersburg PA
CBHW071939210526
45479CB00002B/742